Dancing Lights of the North

by Linda Bullock

Thousands of years ago, a group of **astronomers** looked into the night sky and saw a breathtaking sight. The sky was glowing with colors that stretched like shimmering curtains across the darkness. The astronomers, or people who study objects in space, carved symbols into wet tablets of clay to describe their observations. What they saw would later become known as the Northern Lights.

Neither those astronomers nor other people who saw the lights understood what they were. The Inuit people of Alaska told their children that the lights were the spirits of the seals, salmon, deer, and whales they hunted, all dancing across the sky. To the people of Northern Europe, the lights were a reflection of the fire that they believed surrounded the oceans of the world.

Ancient people created legends to explain Northern Lights.

The sun flings out solar wind particles much like a sprinkler throws out water droplets.

Today, scientists understand what the Northern Lights are, and how they are formed. It all begins with the Sun, which is actually a glowing ball of gases. The heat deep within the Sun is so great that it causes the tiniest bits of a gas, called **atoms**, to break apart into even tinier particles, each full of electrical energy. This energy makes the particles move, and they move with so much speed that they escape the Sun's **gravity**, or pull. A stream of particles moving away from the sun is called a **solar wind**.

The particles fly outward into space and past the planets. When they get near Earth, something unexpected happens. Earth has an iron core, or center, which acts like an enormous magnet. This magnet pulls the solar winds in toward Earth. They enter the upper **atmosphere**, which is the layer of air surrounding Earth, where they crash into air **molecules**, or groups of atoms. The crash creates energy, which shows up in the form of light. Billions of tiny flashes of light occur at once, creating the Northern Lights.

Solar particles enter Earth's atmosphere and crash into air molecules. The crash creates energy, which shows up as light.

The Northern Lights are one of the most spectacular shows on Earth.

Most people think of the Northern Lights as something very rare, but they actually dance across the sky throughout the year. It is only at night when we can see them, though, and they are more visible the further north you go. Violet, blue, and red lights appear closest to Earth's surface, while higher up, bright green lights fill the sky. Higher still, the lights are ruby red.

The lights also tend to be stronger at certain times of the year, when activity on the Sun is at its peak. That's why the town of Yellowknife, at the edge of the Arctic, attracts thousands of people every winter. During those months, the town sits almost frozen in the extreme cold of Canada's Northwest Territories. But the visitors don't care. Bundled in warm clothes, they sit outside in temperatures that are often well below zero, waiting for the remarkable show called the Northern Lights.